THOUGHT-PROVOKING ARCHITECTURAL DESIGN IDEAS

BY
MAGIC MASON

Copyright © 2024 by Magic Mason

All rights reserved. This book or any of its portion may not be reproduced or transmitted in any means, electronic or mechanical, including recording, photocopying, or by any information storage and retrieval system, without the prior written permission of the copyright holder except in the case of brief quotations embodied in critical reviews and other noncommercial uses permitted by copyright law.

Printed in the United States of America
Library of Congress Control Number: 2024920291
ISBN: Softcover   979-8-89518-317-5
        e-Book   979-8-89518-318-2
Published by: WP Lighthouse
Publication Date: 09/24/2024

To buy a copy of this book, please contact:
WP Lighthouse
Phone: +1-888-668-2459
support@wplighthouse.com
wplighthouse.com

In this architectural book, I will discuss the following topics, principles of interior design and exterior design, houses, and making monuments.

CONTENTS

Chapter 1   **DESIGN PRINCIPLES**

Chapter 2   **DESIGN ACCESORS, WINDOWS**

Chapter 3   **WINDOW – TYPES**

Chapter 4   **HOUSES**

Chapter 5   **ARCHITECTURE DESIGNS AND DRAWING BUILDING THE IDEAS AROUND THE WORLD**

CHAPTER 1

DESIGN PRINCIPLES

- Space
- Shape
- Form
- Mass
- Lines
- Texture
- Pattern
- Light
- Color

SPACE

A nice open area between two floors creates a good space.

What is space? Where can you maximize space in your home? Look at occupancy to get the most for you with space. Rooms like Entry, Kitchen, Entertainment areas are more efficient when they have more space.

SPACE

When designing areas like the entry, kitchen, and entertainment room, functionality should be the first consideration. Think of your kitchen, you should consider how often you cook. This will help you decide whether to have small or large kitchen. This should be the same process for the entertainment room. Consider the uses of a small versus large space for entertainment..

SHAPE

What is shape? Most rooms are Square, or Rectangular, Recesses in wall can create storage on opposite side, recesses in ceiling can provide unique shape for Character.

FORM

These are three good examples showing form we see shape and space which create nice design.

What is Form?

In this picture, the table, photographs, and lamp create more form for the space.

FORM

Why is this floor plan unique?

The elements that create form in this room have a unique relationship. They create several forms.

MASS

How is mass created in architecture? Why is it important?

Mass can be created through accent pieces, like in these pictures below.

HORIZONTAL LINE, VERTICAL LINE, ANGULAR LINE

Vertical, horizontal, and angular lines help create a perfect design.

LINES

Straight and curve lines create a nice combination.

TEXTURE

Smooth texture characteristics in this dining room.

What is Texture, and what Texture can it do for the design of house?

Some Textures can be added during construction while other textures can be added during decorating the house.

PATTERN

Different type of patterns. What does pattern do for design? How do tall black lines make the ceiling look taller or how busy looking for design.

PATTERN

The wallpaper pattern, furniture patterns and rugs patterns create an attractive combination.

Herring bone pattern create a unique and unforgettable entry, also accent wall is continued in mud room as well as the outside of house.

EXTERIOR PATTERN

Externals patterns are wonderful examples make a statement of design. They reinforce character and can be very effective if brought inside as well.

LIGHT

Light from the window fills this room used for a family room during the daytime.

Lighting is for function and decoration. Light and relaxation are also related.

LIGHT

Type of Lighting: Direct, Indirect, Accent, Under cabinet, Mood , New LED, White Light, Soft Light, Architectural lighting, Etc.

LIGHT

Architectural lighting is used to fill a contemporary living room with a soft diffused glow.

Lights, Wall plugs, Basic architectural measurement for wall plug, lights placing electrical elements and why?

SUN LIGHT

Good lighting is an essential part of decorating your home.

Notice how the arches in the photos above allow more light into the room.

LIGHT

Design, Direction of light, climate, this fantastic natural lighting feature accompanied by a glass wall to create an open and lighted feel to space.

COLOR

The color wheel.

COLOR WHEEL

Where do you want worm colors VS cold colors?

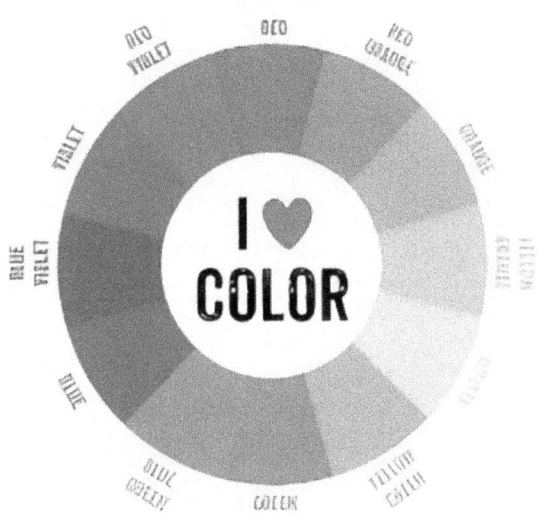

COLOR

Ask these questions when considering these colors:

Why is color so important, how do we view color, how do colors make us feel, what is too much color, and what does color outside VS inside mean?

Color onto wall VS floor VS furniture Art + accent pieces

COLOR MONOCHROMATIC

Color in Pattern VS lines, Choosing complimentary colors schemes.

COLOR

The color contrast in the room is an example of direct compliment of color.

COLOR

Look at the 2 front doors of these similar houses, both are accents that draw attention to the house.

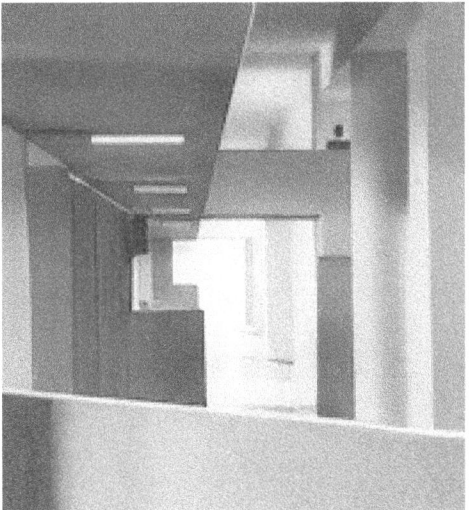

DIRECT COMPLIMENT COLOR

Split level colors are very complimentary. Great example of chain rail + color selection to create this rich space especially with the stub wall.

MONOCHROMATIC COLOR

In these 2 monochromatic photos imagine your furniture in these spaces, would you change the color?

While softer colors can ease the contrast and may be good for a relaxing space.

EXTERIOR COLOR

COLOR

Accent wall, why, how?

COLOR+TEXTURE BRINGS EXCITEMENT

SPLIT COMPLEMENT

Lets talk about split complement and how it can be used.

TRIADIC COMPLEMENTS

ANALOGOUS

COLORS AND FREEDOM OF DESIGN

COLOR

Why is color important to culture? How to design the flags, How people respond to colors.

EXAMPLE OF COLOR BLUES, GREENS, AND WHITES

COLOR RELAXATION

What does color mean for relaxation, why is it important to relax?

CHAPTER 2

DESIGN PRINCIPLES

- Scale
- Proportion
- Balance
- Rhythm
- Emphasis
- Harmony

SCALE

With a good size of scale, we can see better elements of design. Architectural statement VS function should be considered.

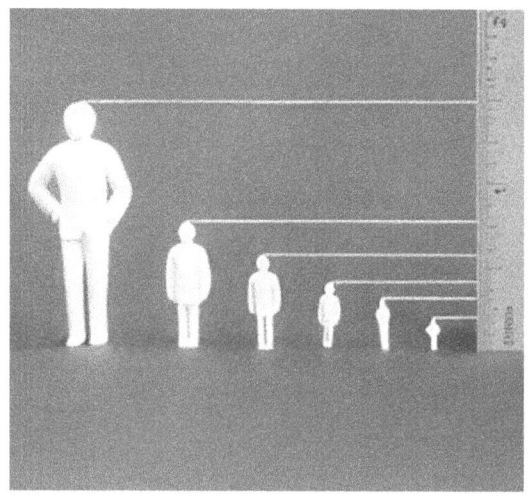 

SCALE

Drawing spaces with scale we can see size of person with space around the design, top view shows sizes, we can see how easily can move around.

The illustration above shows how we can use scale rules to draw 20 feet for example for just 5 inches in scale of ¼.

  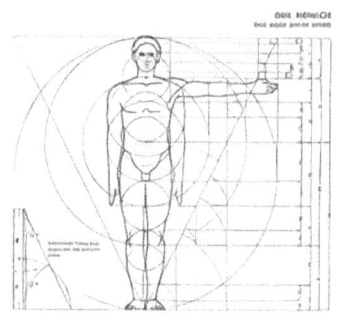

EXTERIOR SCALES

How big is your lot? How and why is it important to see scale of the job before constructing the actual building?

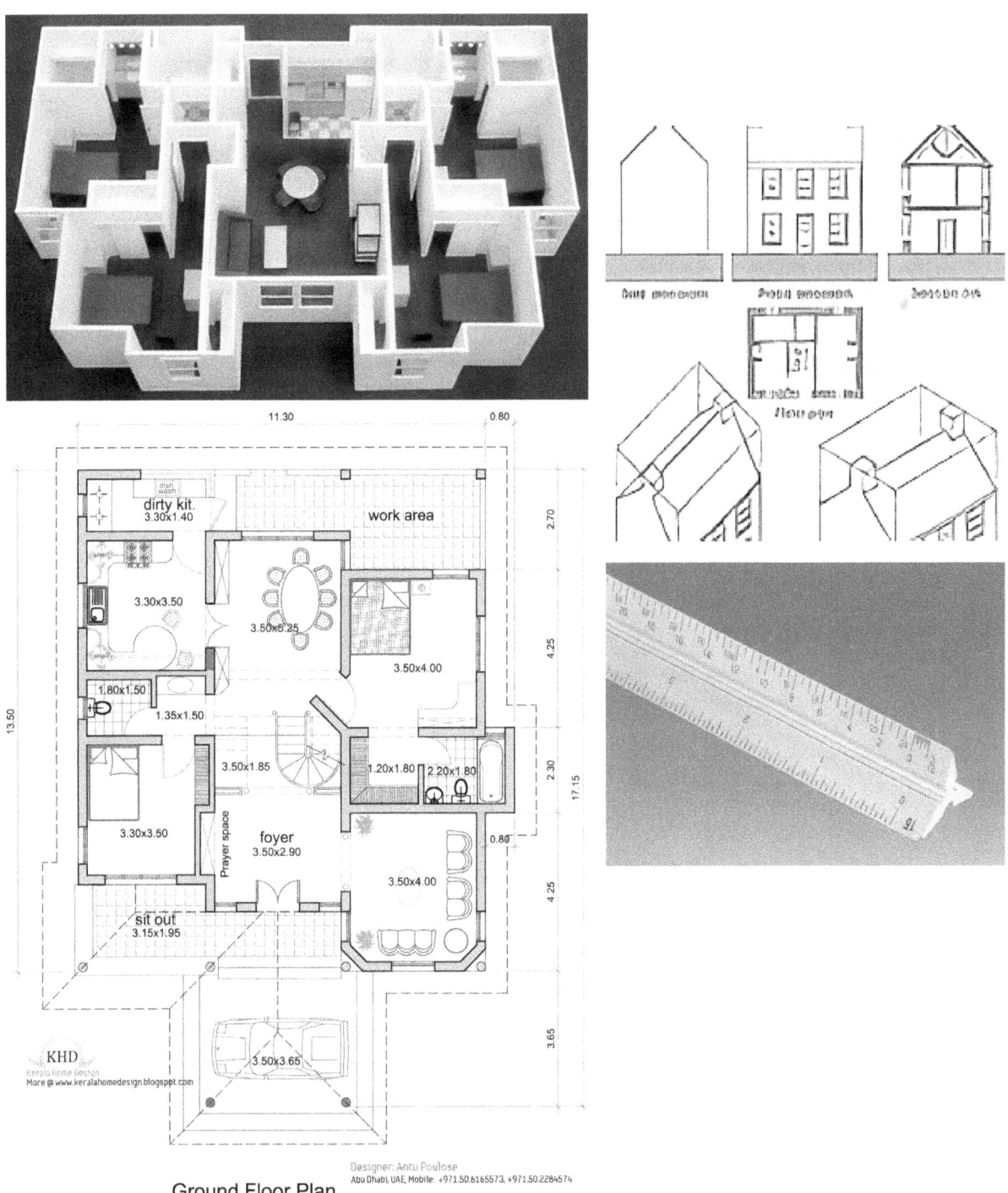

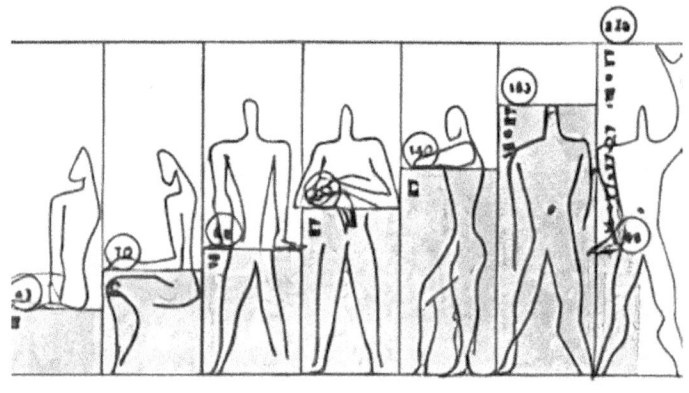

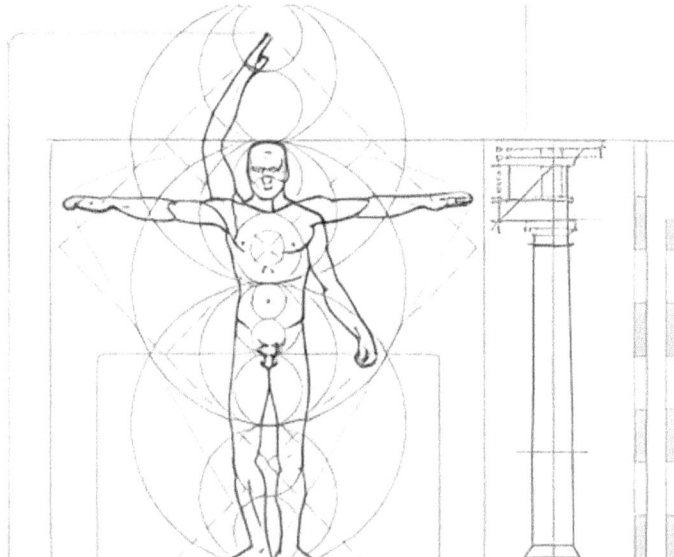

PROPORTION

Use body basis in proportion to view space with proper scale.

PROPORTION IN DESIGN

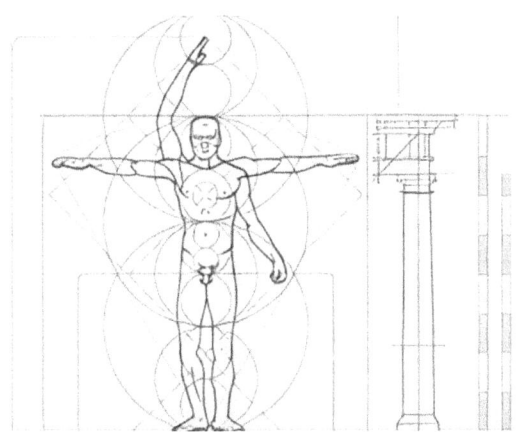

Interior, Exterior

FINDING THE BALANCE

Discovering balance is always challenging.

BALANCE

Here are few samples of balance, Symmetrical, Non-symmetrical and Radial.

RADIAL BALANCE

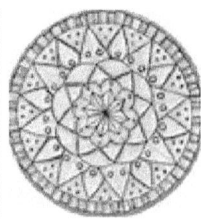

INTERIOR RHYTHM

What is Rhythm in Architecture design, why is important to an intuit Rhythm?

EXTERIOR RHYTHM

Examples of Exterior Rhythm.

EMPHASIS

The photos below illustrate the importance of emphasis in architecture

Is this a real fireplace, Architectural VS. T.V decorative?

HARMONY

HARMONY

HARMONY

Why is it important to have a harmony in architecture design, how do scale, proportion, balance, rhythm, tie to this space together give points on both pictures?

CHAPTER 3

DESIGN ACCESSORIES

Window – Types

BLINDS

ROMAN SHADES, CURTAIN

DECORATIVE RODS

WINDOWS

Bay window, Kitchen window

WINDOWS

Arched windows and Bay windows

VERTICAL VENATION BLINDS, ROMAN SHADES

WINDOW TREATMENTS

Example of windows treatments.

FLOORING

Examples of Flooring, ceramic tile and hardwood and example of medallion.

FLOORING
What can good flooring do for a home?

BRICK AND STONE FLOOR

What is important of this flooring character?

Tile, Stone, Concrete, wooden, carpet, Laminate, Vinyl sheet, or vinyl tiles what are the benefits of each materials? Looks, Durability, Hardness, moisture, used, Etc.

STONE AND WOOD FLOORING

Example of Slate, or stone tiles and Vinyl sheets.

CERAMIC TILE

Examples of tiling backsplash in kitchen.

FURNITURE

Few examples of space and furniture in rooms

FURNITURE

Few examples, of Modern furniture.

FURNITURE STYLES

Example of chairs from different design styles.

FURNITURE FROM PAST TO PRESENT

How we can coordinate the design of furniture with our plan.

FURNITURE PATTERNS

What about pattern in furniture, what they do to design the room?

Vessel

FURNITURE THINKER

How we can think to design the furniture in room.

FURNITURE

Louis XIV

Louis XV

Louis XVI

Renaissance

Regency

Modern

LOUIS XV

Example of furniture during Louis 15th

XVI
Examples of Louis 16th

XVI

Examples of Louis 16th furniture

RENAISSANCES
Examples of renaissances furniture

BED ROOMS

Few examples of modern furniture.

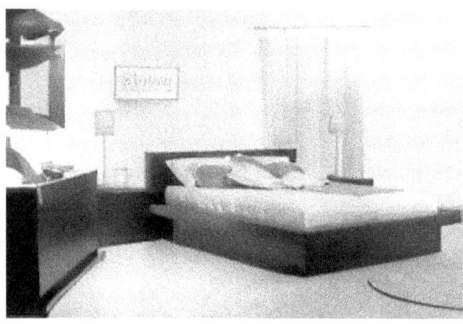  

19TH CENTURY FURNITURE

Furniture of 19th century

20TH CENTURY

20th century and modern design.

21ST CENTURY

Examples of modern design furniture.

CHAPTER 4

DESIGNING HOUSES AND BUILDINGS

Few examples of houses in different clement one with flat roof one with the gable roof.

FEW EXAMPLES OF CUTE HOUSES

Modern design and traditional design.

One room house

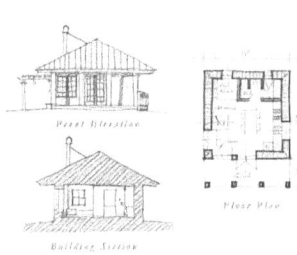

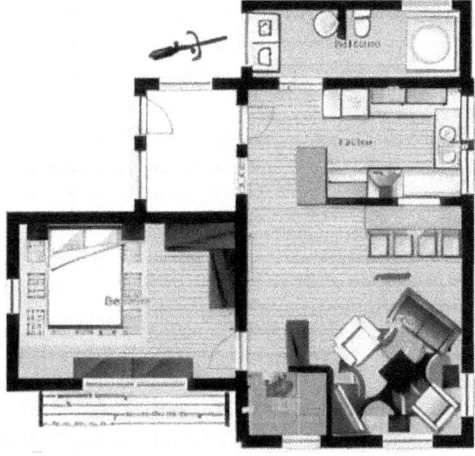

It can be houses or offices.

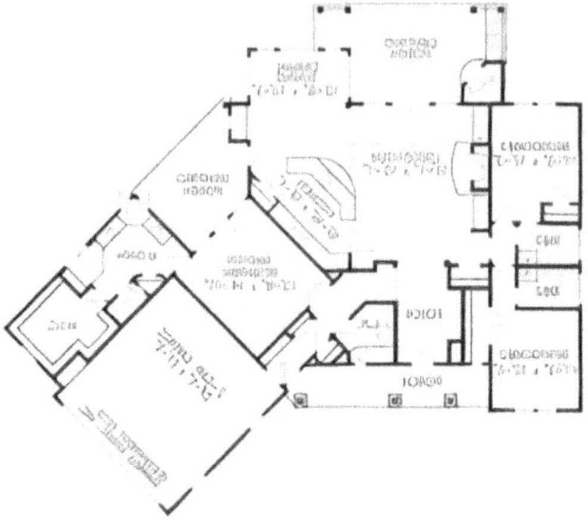

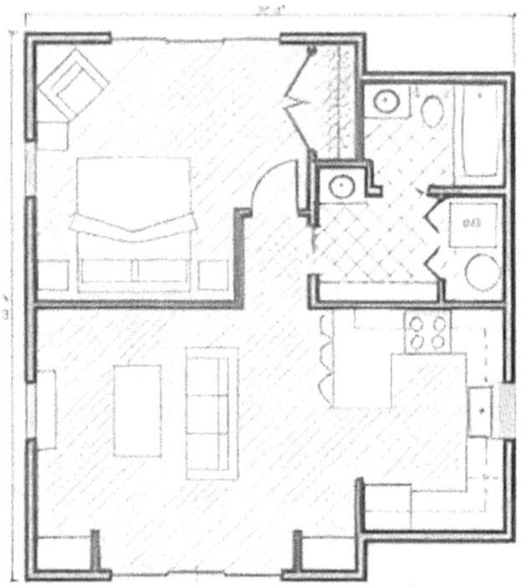

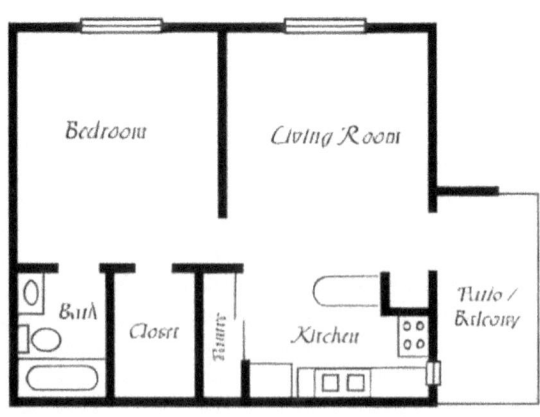

Apartments house with a big balcony.

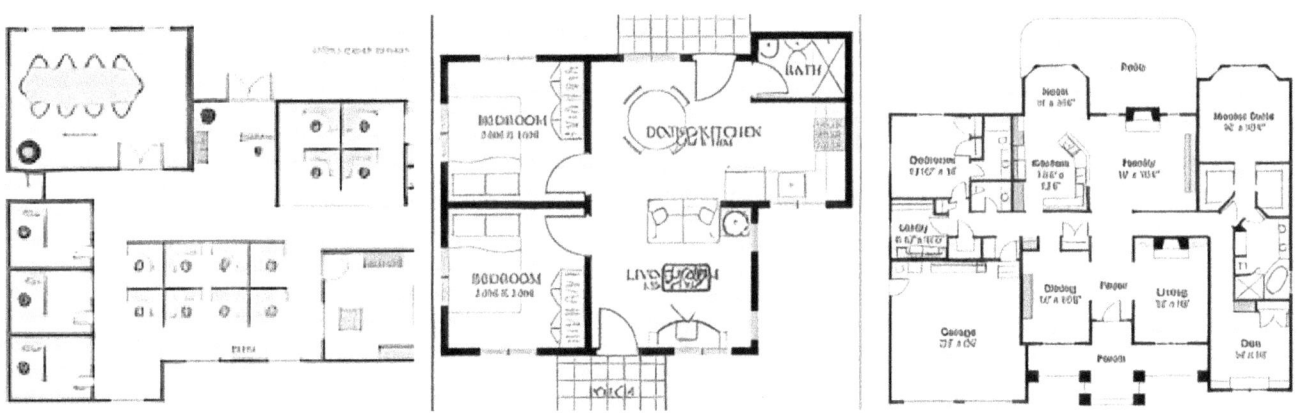

GOOD DESIGN

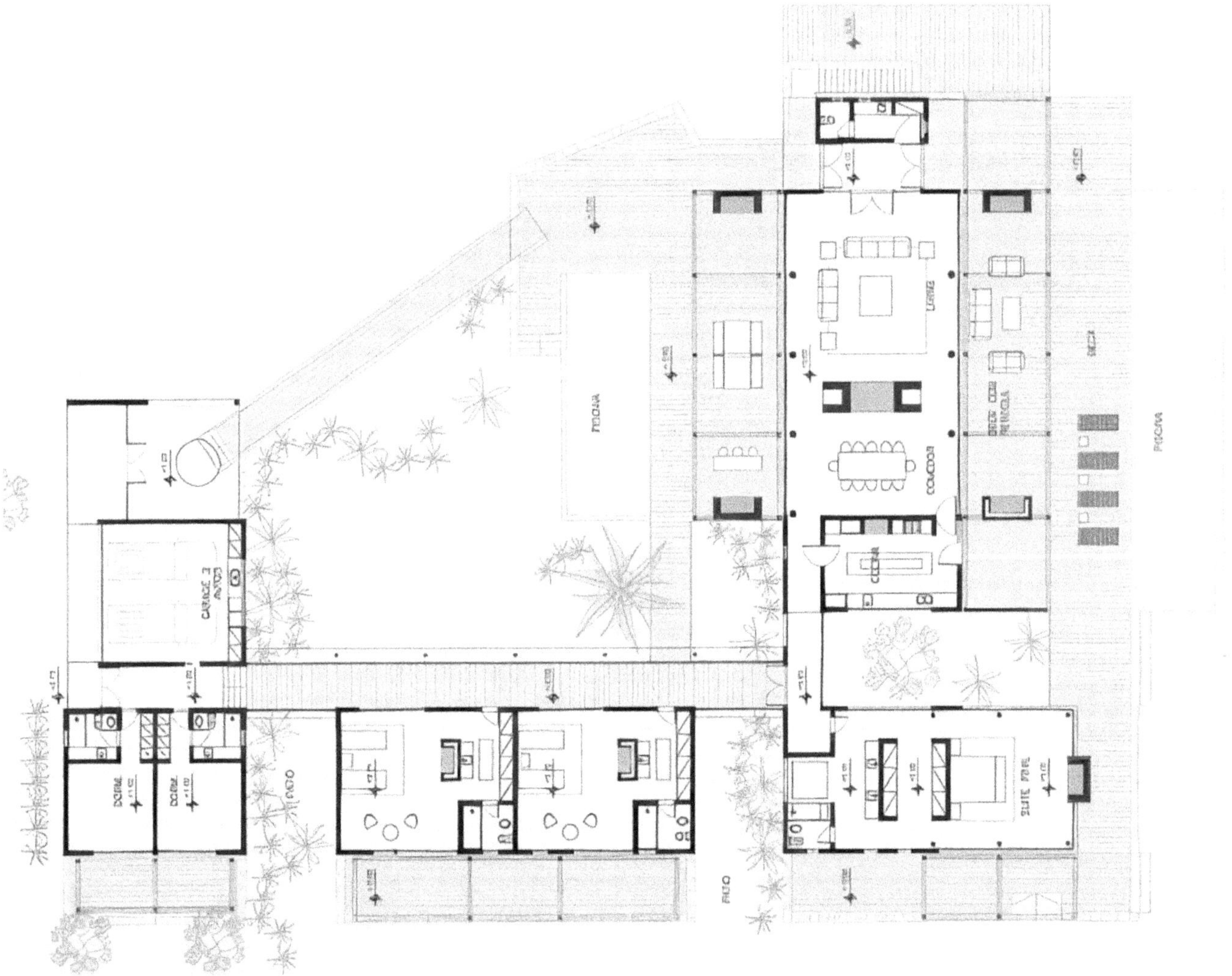

GETTING STARTED WITH FREEDOM AND SENSES

DRAWING ARCHITECTURE DESIGN

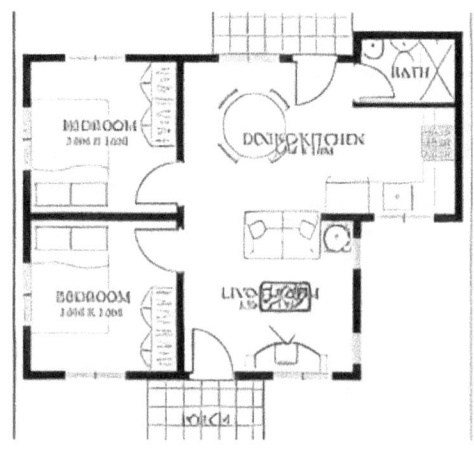
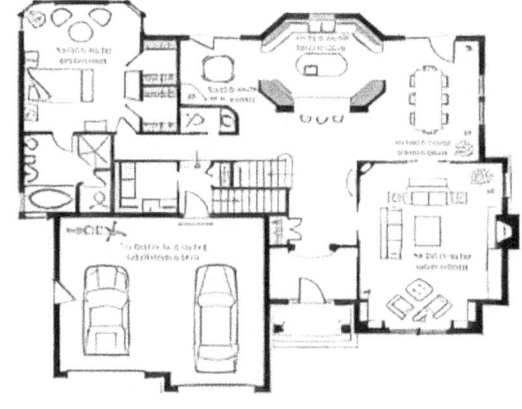

DRAFTING TABLE

We need table and some drafting tools to start the drawing or blueprint for our plan, we need the tape measuring tools to measure the land and building to add rooms or redesign our house.

PLAN AND ELEVATION

To draw in scale usually we scale it down to 100 times smaller to actual size.

For example, 10 feet to 1 inch and 60 feet to 6 inches. Elevation is measurement of height of buildings and view of front or back of the house, with scale.

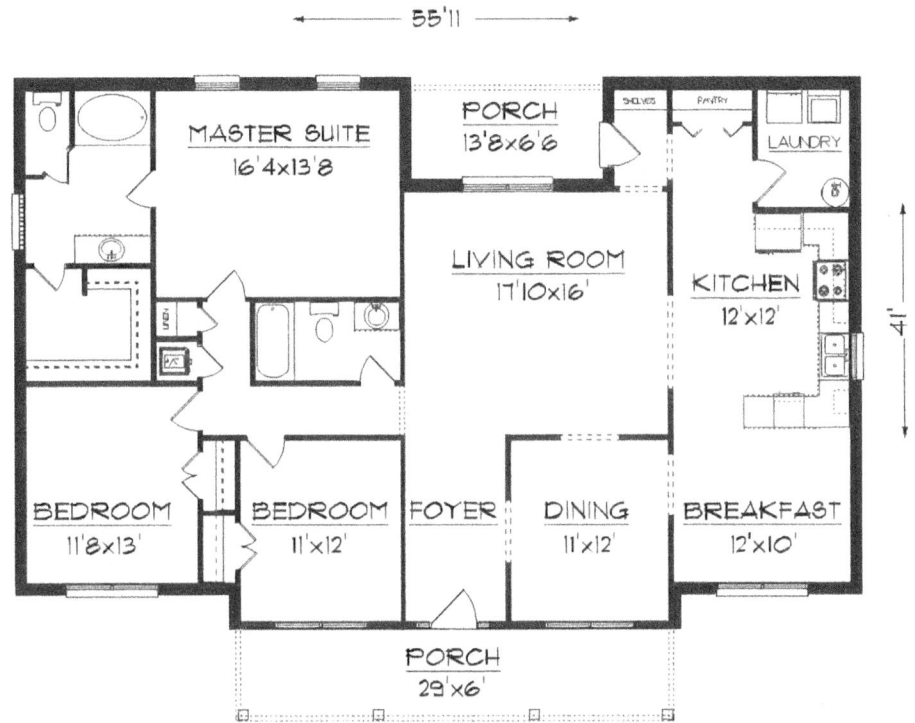

ELEVATION IS A VIEW OF FRONT, SIDE OF OBJECT, PLAN OR BUILDING

SITE PLAN

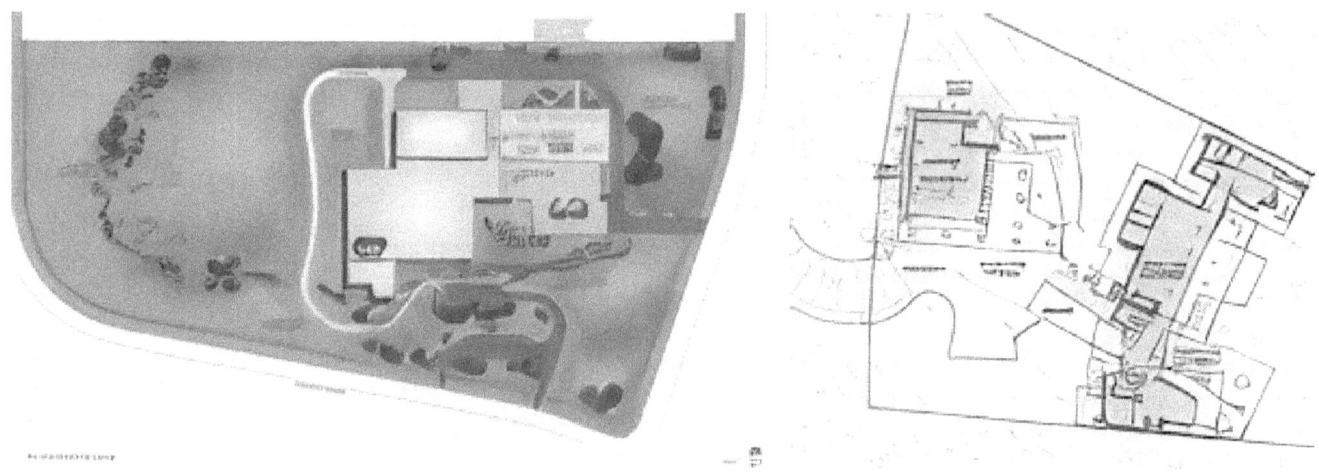

Site plan must show of the dimension from street and neighbors and usually scale 400 times smaller than house plan and must shows which way is north.

FOUNDATION PLAN

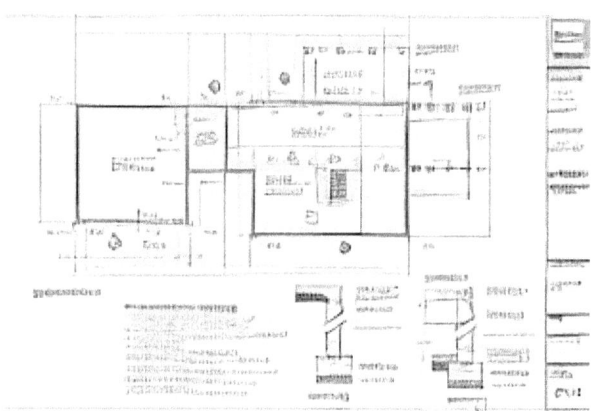

1st plan used to construct of any building is foundation plan, which is almost floor plan with an extended wall of building or column in the ground bigger than thickness of wall or column.

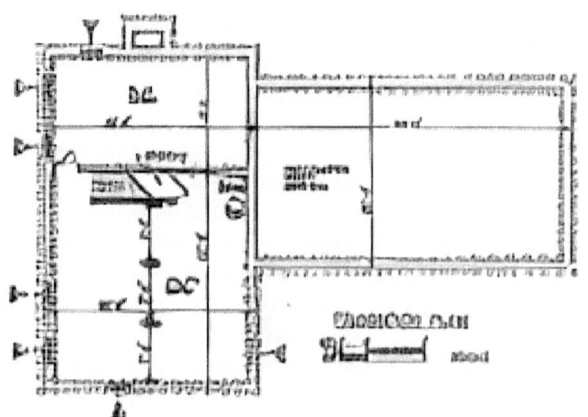

ROOF PLAN

Usually we need to plan the roof plan in any construction of residential or commercial Building.

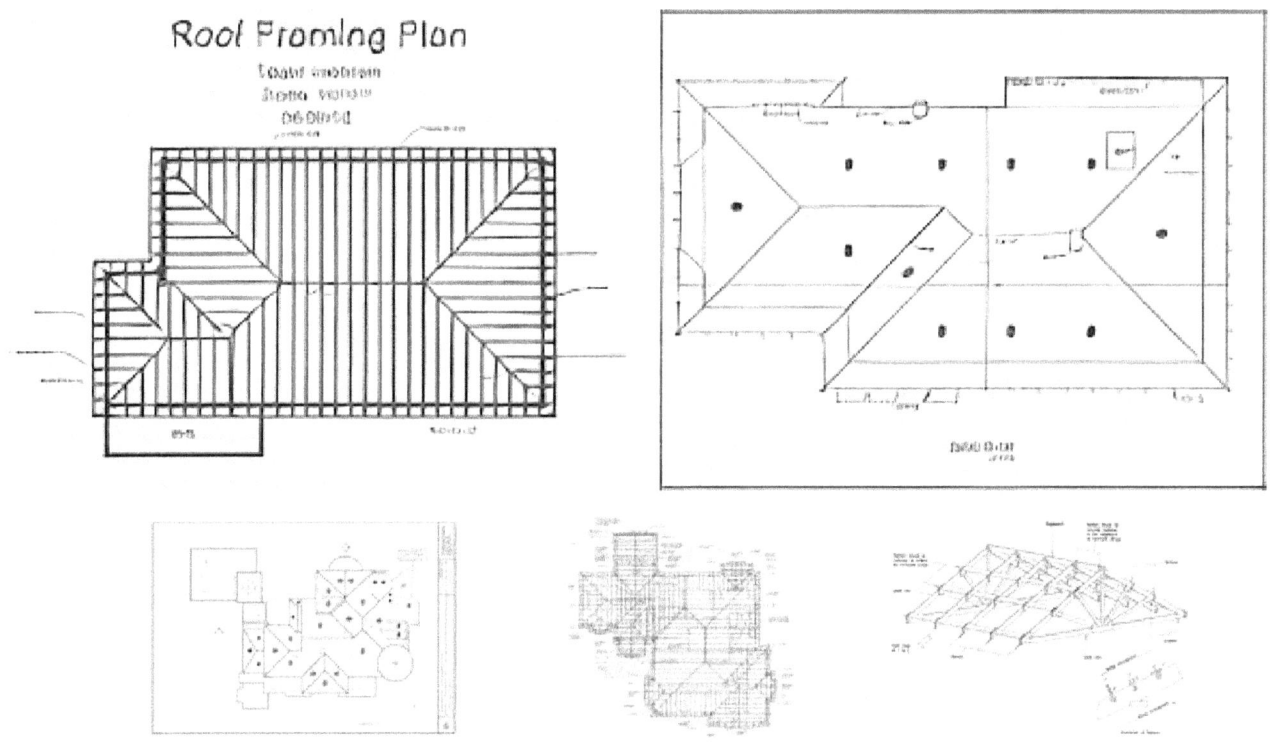

FLOOR PLAN, SECTION, DETAILS, ELEVATION

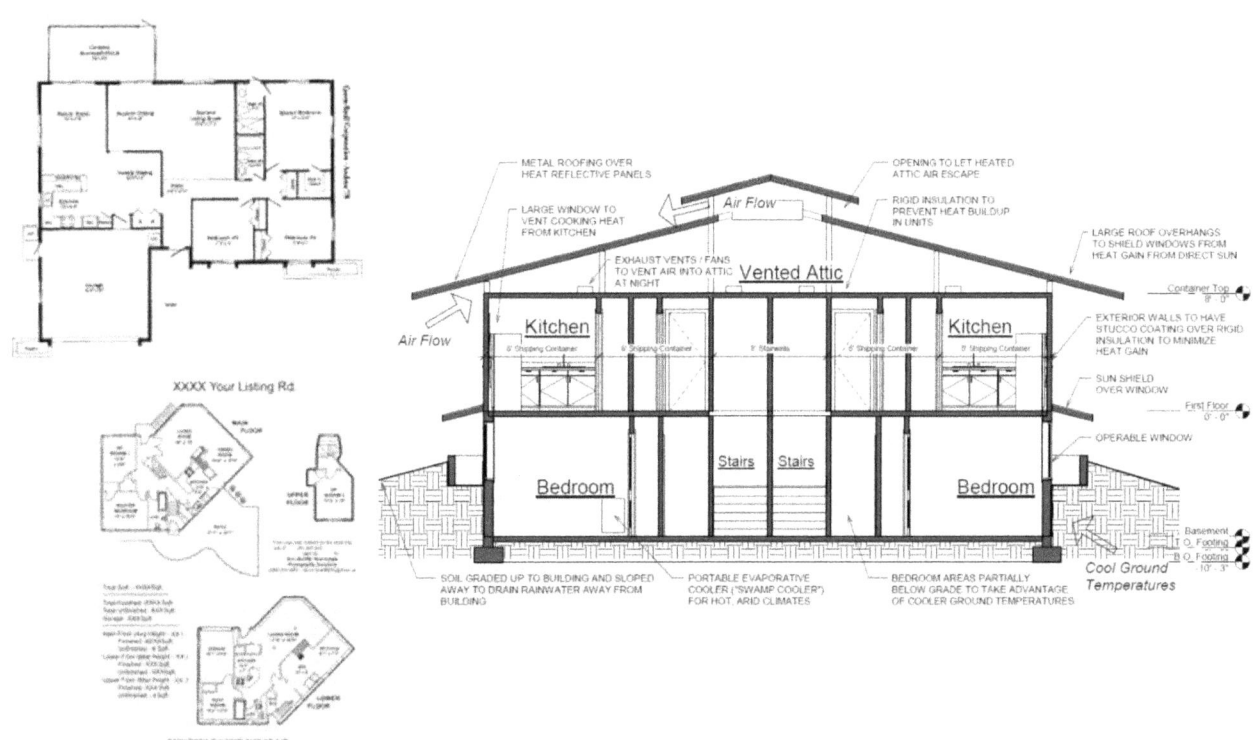

NORTH SIGN

Every plan we draw we must show the north in plan or in blueprint.

These are some examples of direction of north in drawing and we must draw the plan in north direction. All of the sheet of drawing must have north design.

ELECTRIC PLAN

All plan we do for additional room or house plan, we must have an electrical plan that is presented and approved by the city government.

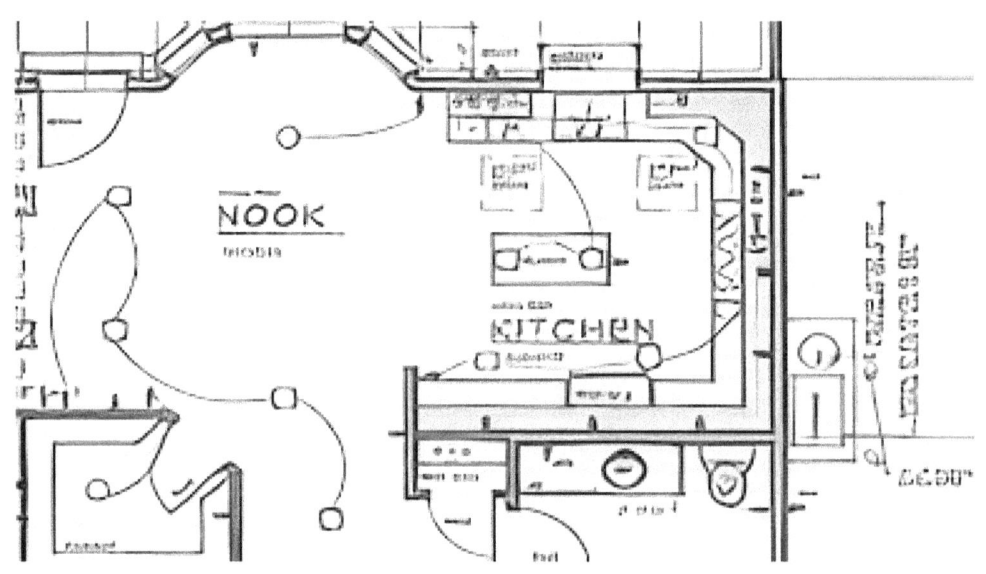

These are some examples of details of corners or some part of the house We design or for additional which we must show the city how the attach to the other part of building and shows the all materials we are going to use.

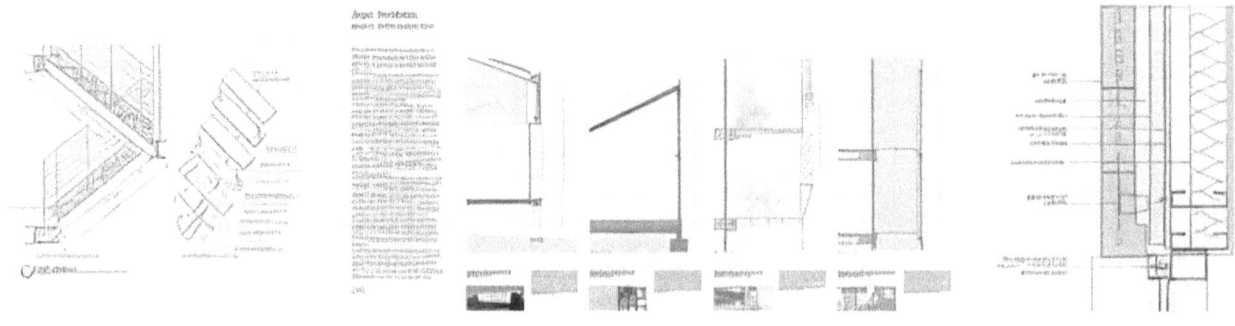

HOUSE PLAN

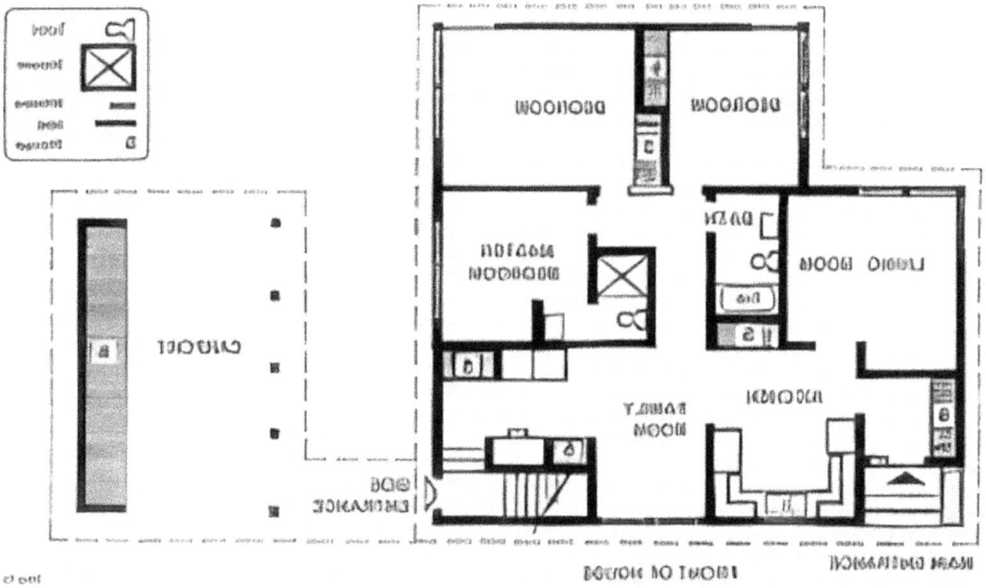

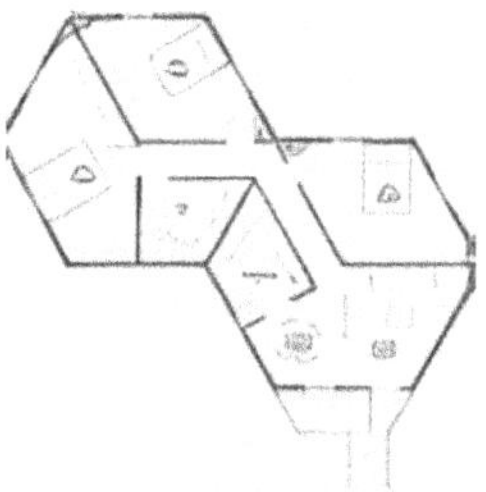

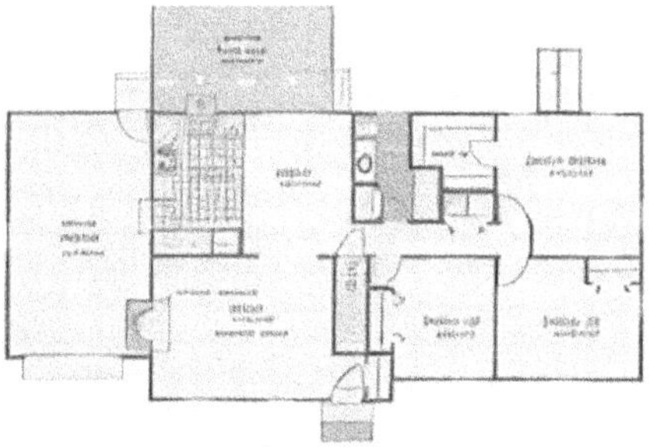

Few examples of house plans

HOUSE PLAN

One example of expensive house plan

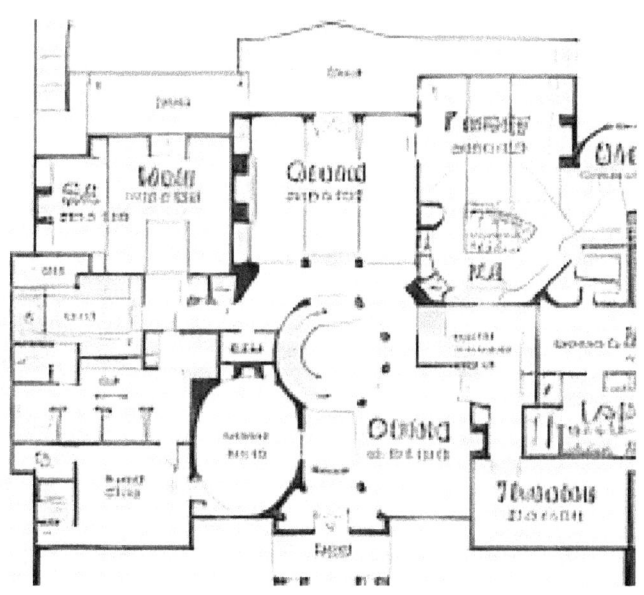

HOUSE PLAN

Few house plans

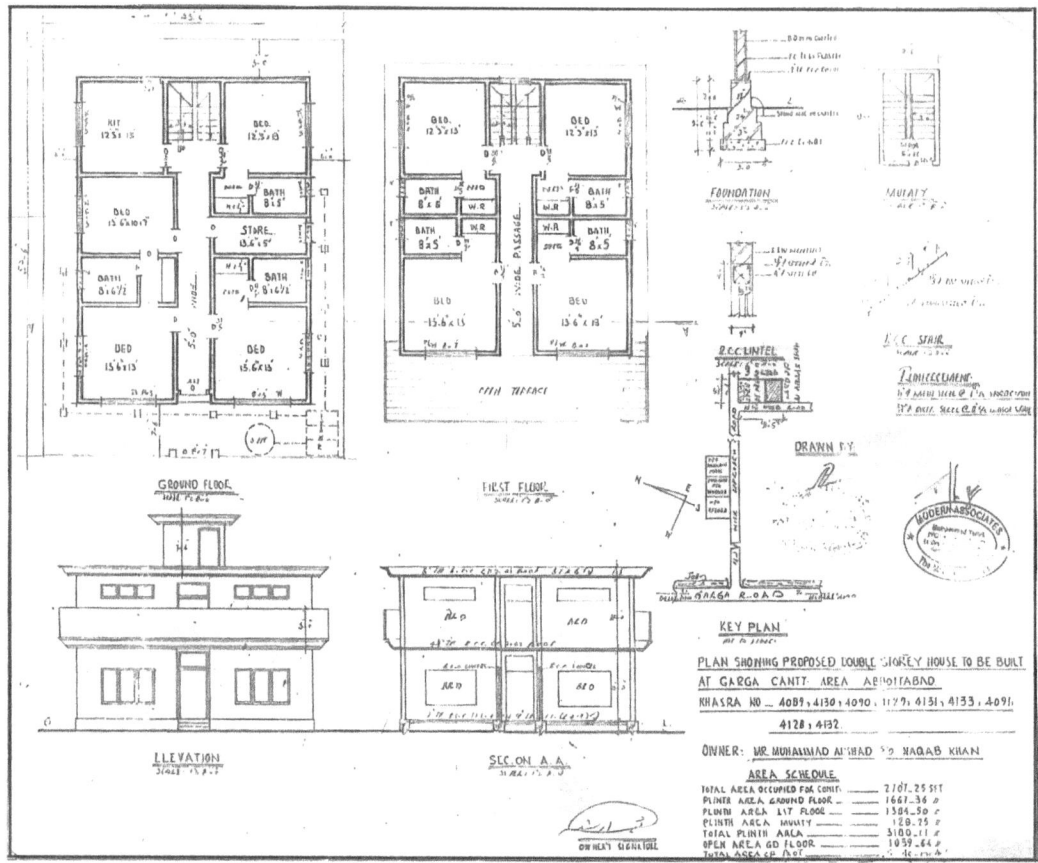

HOUSE PLAN

2 bedroom house plan with one bathroom

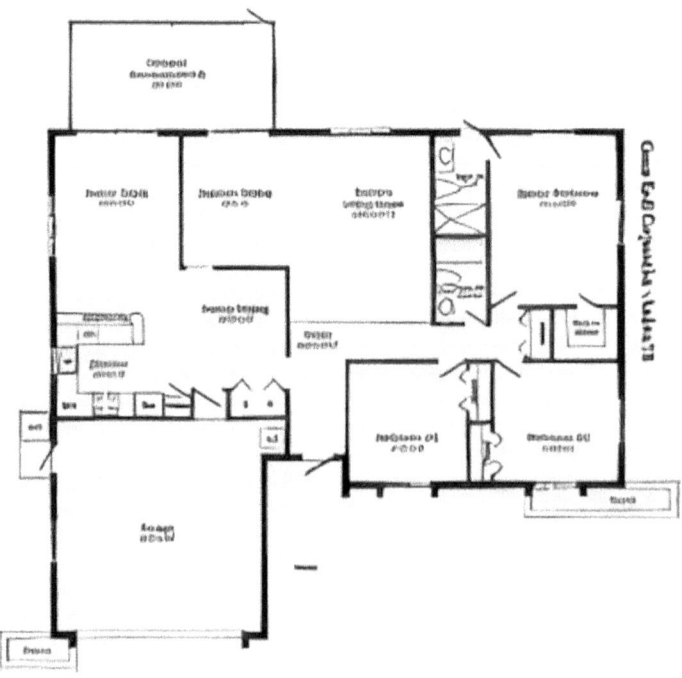

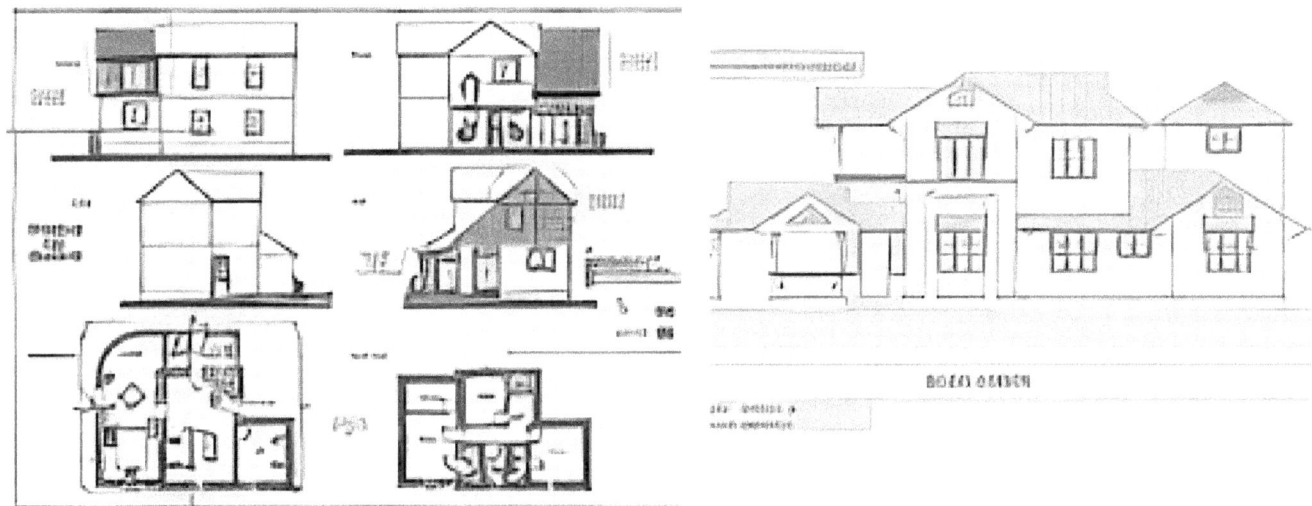

Several exterior photos elevation of houses small VS big

CITY PLAN AND HOUSE PERMIT

For city we need all floor plans, for example 1st floor second floor.

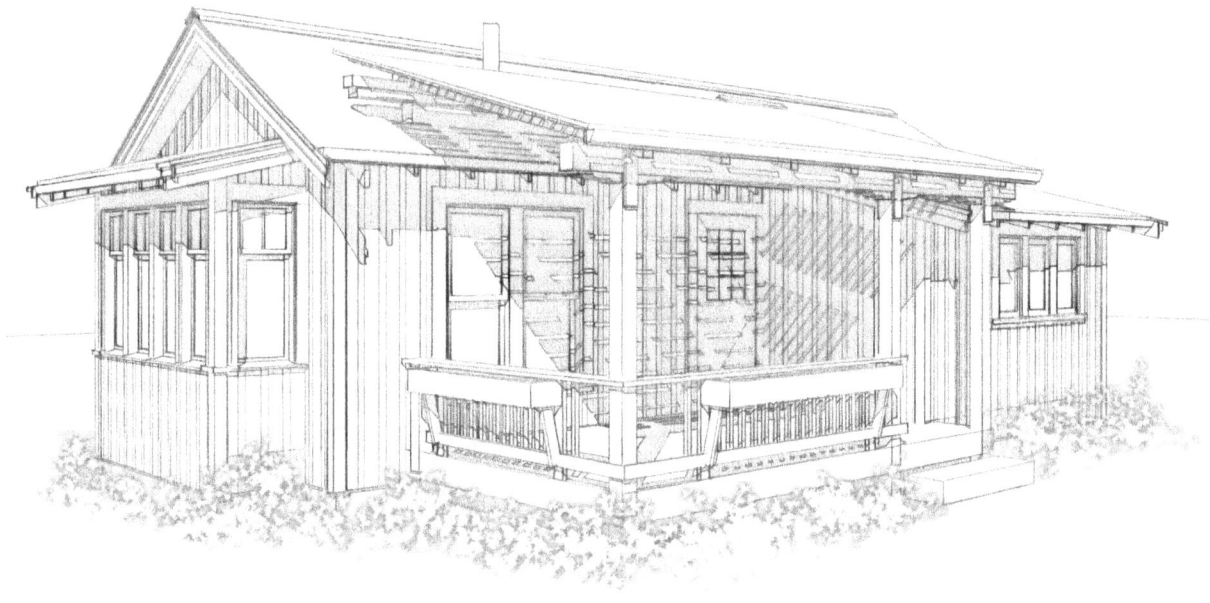

CITY PLAN HOUSE PERMIT SHEETS

Example of one sheet drawing of floor plan with elevation and section in one sheet.

ONE POINT PERSPECTIVES

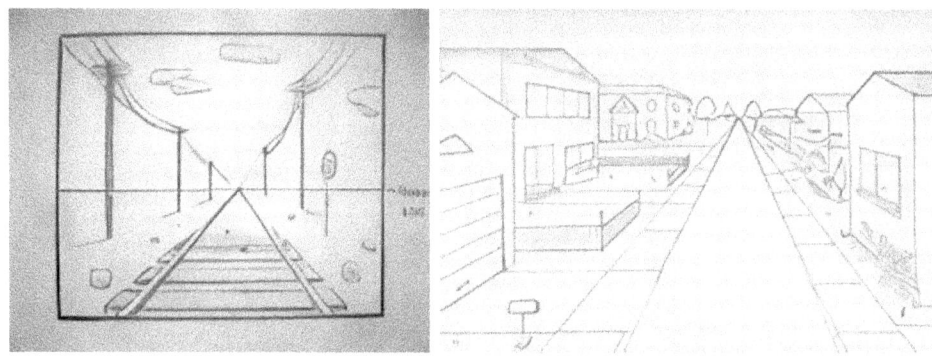

Perspective usually is for your interest and city not need it any perspective of your building, perspective are, one point which is you see in above picture.

ONE POINT PERSPECTIVE

Few more example of one point perspective which all objects go to one point of view.

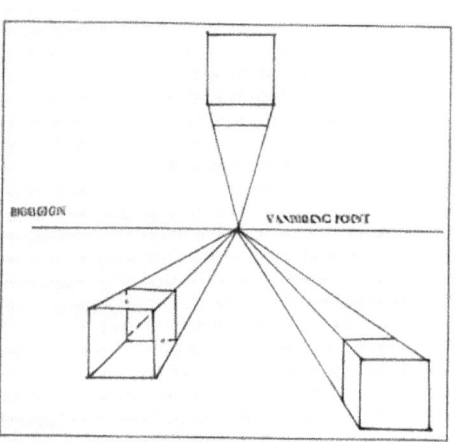

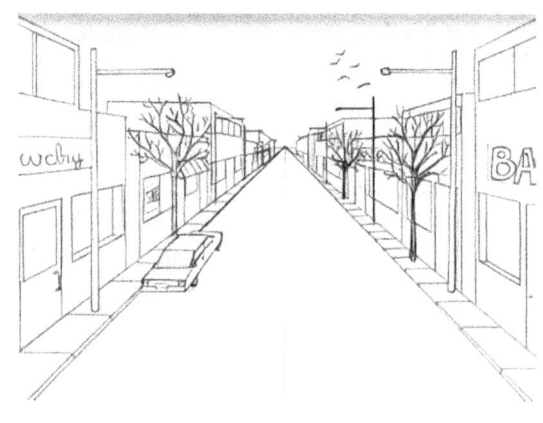

TWO POINT PERSPECTIVES

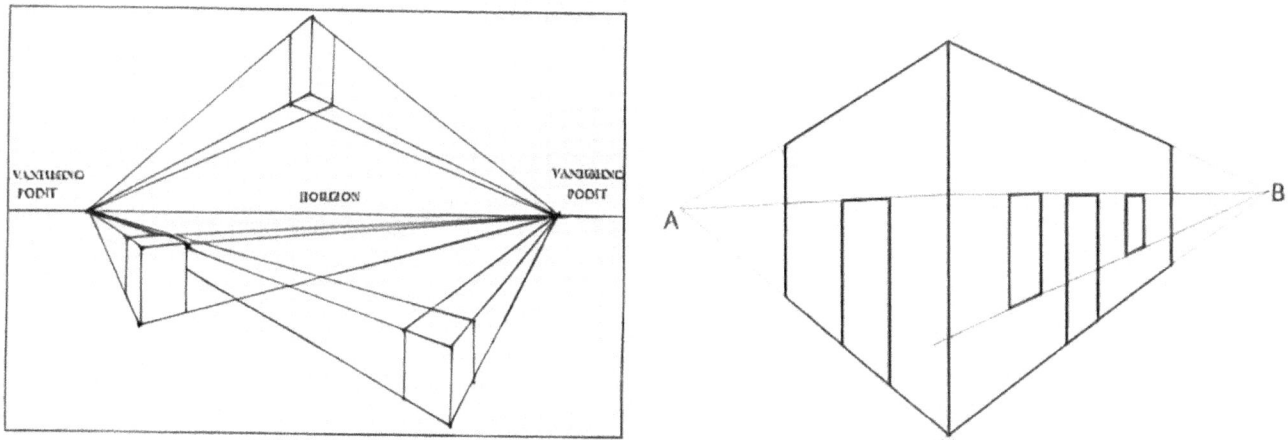

Second perspective are two points perspectives which you see in above pictures.

TWO POINT PERSPECTIVES

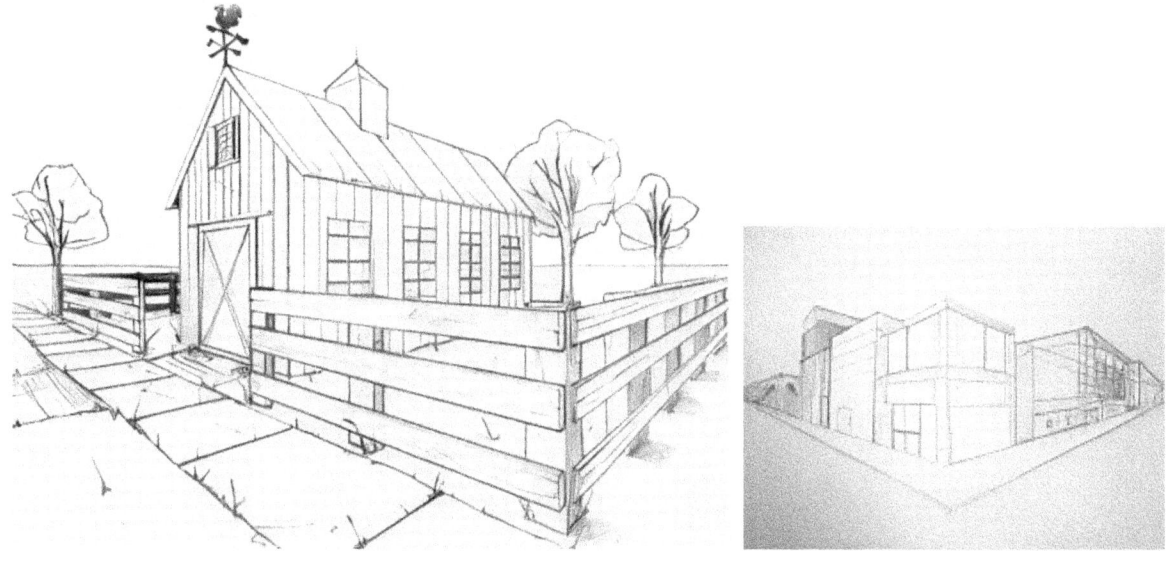

More examples of two point perspectives

TWO POINT PERSPECTIVES

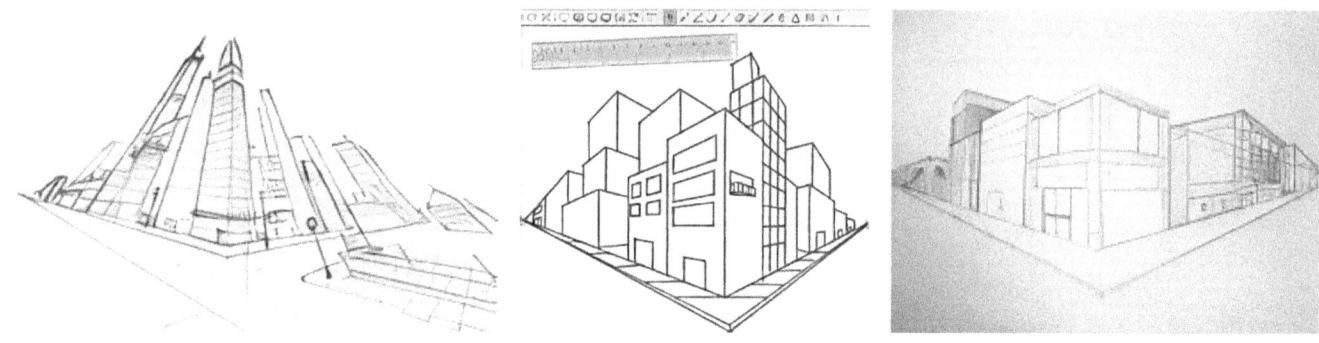

Examples of two point perspectives.

THREE POINT PERSPECTIVES

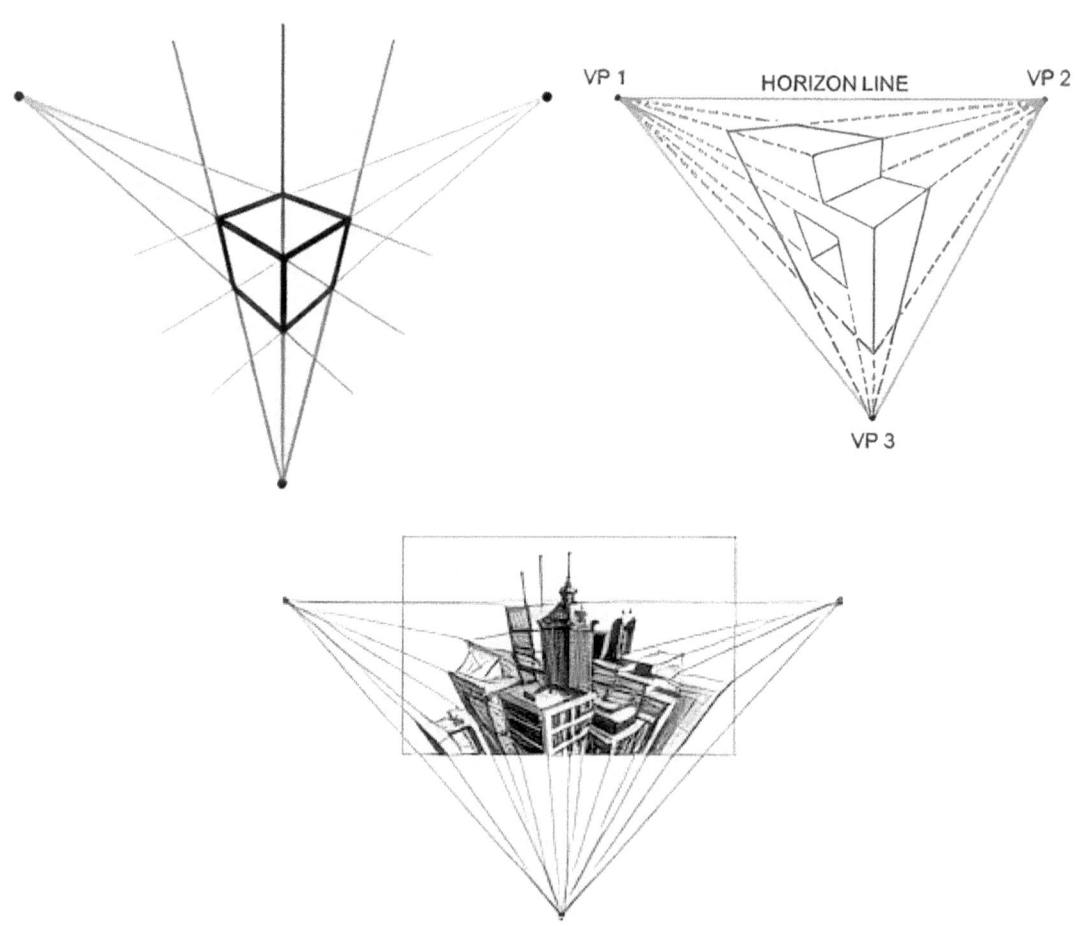

3rd kind of perspective are three points perspectives which have height goes to infinity too or to the point.

THREE POINT PERSPECTIVES

3 DIFFERENT PERSPECTIVE DRAWING METHOD

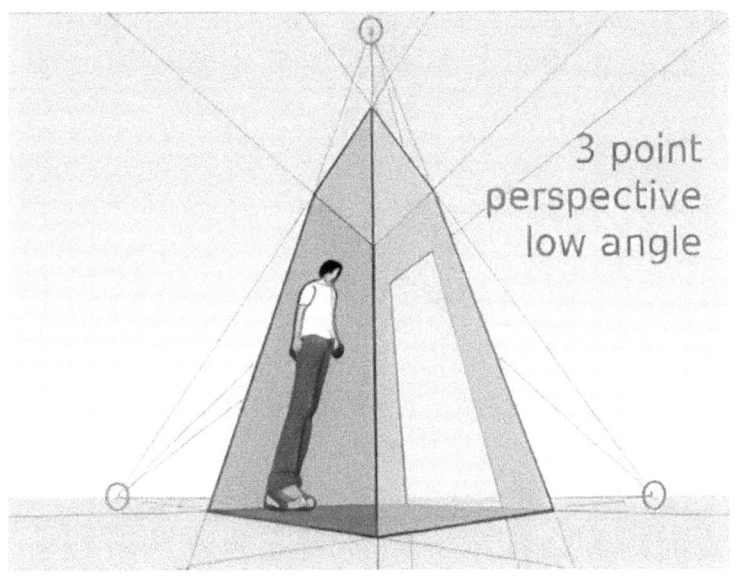

CHAPTER 5

ARCHITECTURE, DESIGNS, AND IDEAS FROM AROUND THE WORLD

Creating architecture from around the world from houses to monuments

MONUMENTS CREATED WITH NEW IDEAS

CONSTRUCTION OF FREEDOM IDEAS

A TO Z IDEAS

Symmetrical Windows and FirePlace

Nice house design

Details of walls and floors

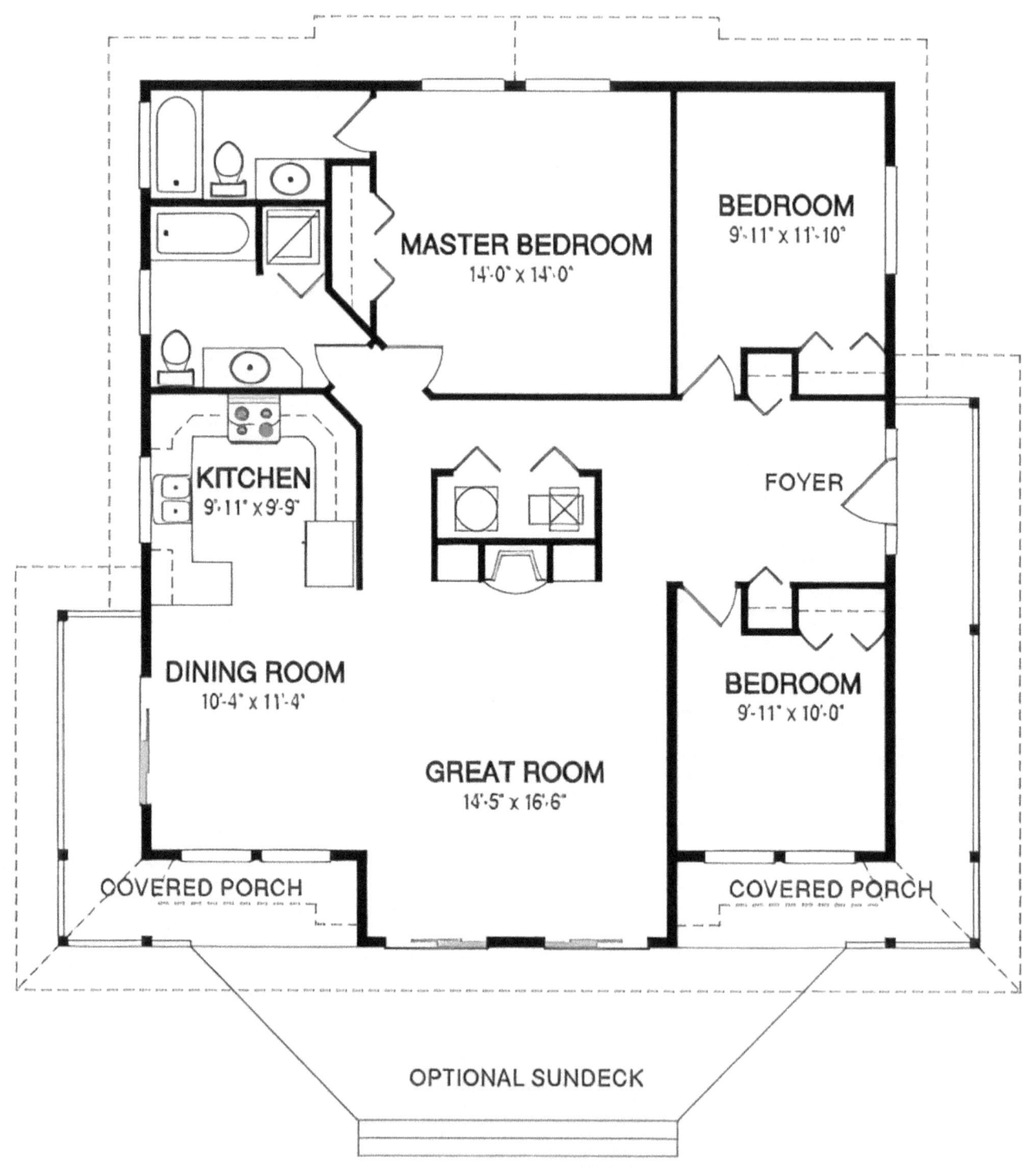

Brick, New solution to disaster in north America

Building Residential houses from Foundation to Roof with Brick.

I will demonstrate build the foundation to wall all with brick. This way materials all heavy and is strong, wind, rain, and hurricanes cannot damage the structure.

I will start with some pictures and details which all explains the details of how to do the job.

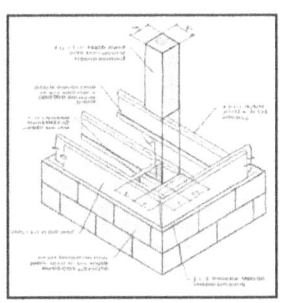
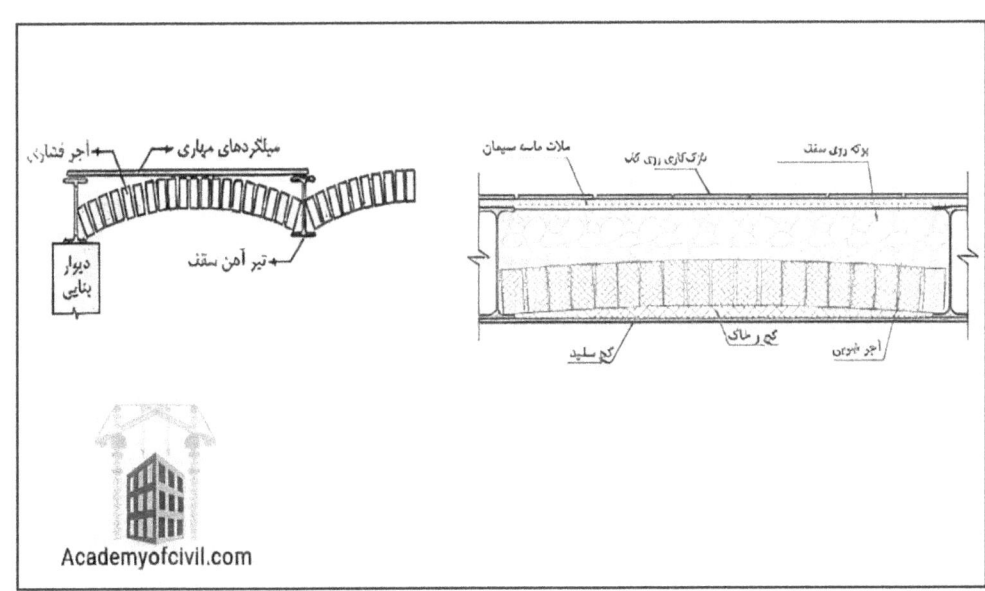

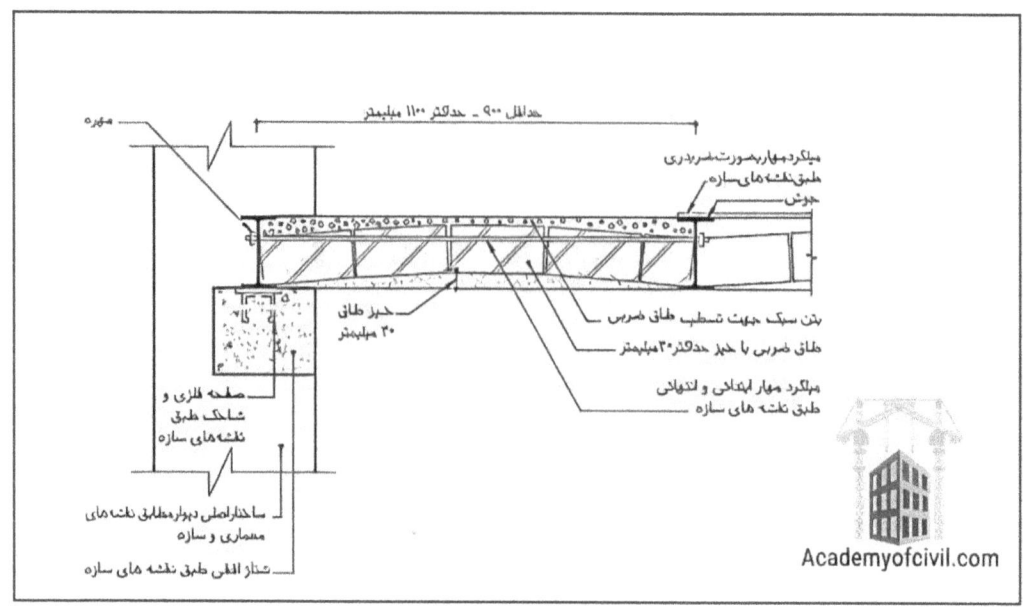

Brick manufacturing can be redesigned for new bricks. Bricks Must be very cheap and not needed stack or bended in package can be loaded in big truck and dumped in site. Bricks bust made of clay and limestone with high heat also very light. Shape square 4x10 inches. If bricks are dumped in site even some broken can be used in small pieces used in the construction job.

Mortar we needed for lay down the foundation are Portland cement for wall with mix of sand and some soil.

Mortar for ceiling bricks must be clay and gravel. We must be mix first dry. Mortar must be ½ gravel, ½ fine clay soil. We must have with big pots or tray or tub, fist fill half tub with water. with two hands spread the mix of gravel and clay over the water. until the tub we will fill. tub not to big we can lift. we must lift over scuffle.

IS ARCHITECTURE IS ART?

About the Author

Magic Mason was born in Tehran, Iran, U.S. Citizen with diverse international experience. Doctor of Philosophy, General Psychology in progress. Master of Public Administration, Bachelor of Science in Industrial Technology and Construction Management, from Northern Kentucky University, USA

Business Owner, Greater Cincinnati, Ohio area, 2004- 2015.

- Author/ Inventor, Legal Concept of the Law and Human Behavior Senses. Amazon.com Published 2009.
- Author of World Language published 2017.
- Invented political Chess Game: an expansion of classic chess designed to help children learn about political systems.(patent, 2006).

Creator of the "super Bed" to reduce heating and cooling expenses. (Patent, 2009).

Architecture Can Be Fun and Create Good Career in All over the World.